SHORT BACK & SIDEWAYS

POEMS & PROSE

HONE TUWHARE

GODWIT

Published by Godwit Press Limited,
44 Ellerton Road, Mount Eden,
Auckland 4, New Zealand

© Hone Tuwhare 1992
First published 1992
Reprinted 1992
Printed in Singapore

National Library of New Zealand
Cataloguing-in-Publication data

Tuwhare, Hone, 1922–
   Short back & sideways / Hone Tuwhare. Auckland, N.Z.:
Godwit Press, 1992.
   1 v.
   Poems and prose.
   ISBN 0–908877–20–X
   I. Title. II. Title: Short back & sideways.
   NZ 821.2

The publishers acknowledge the assistance
of the Literature Programme of the
Queen Elizabeth II Arts Council of New Zealand.

Contents

Preface: At the lodge

(by Rewi Tamakuru Tuwhare)

That bit of four-by-two you lift down, de-nail and
hammer, came from a tree which took maybe twenty years
to grow: now it's going to be part of a verandah
or a wooden step.

The concrete mixer that churns out wet concrete
has a part in the scheme of things, too; sand
water and cement make a solid foundation
for a space-age Country Lodge.

The half dozen goats who chew grass endlessly
shit on the newly mown lawns or try to climb the walls
of the empty swimming pool:

The two dogs chase bits of wood I throw away from
them and fetch and retrieve them salivating at the mouth
to drop them at my feet.

The hungry chooks flutter and squawk at me after I feed
them with small brown pellets from a large paper bag.
Cracks appear

in the sun-baked earth — the lawn sprinkled with
yellow daisies, the swimming pool that will never
be filled:

'I heard thunder and lightning in my heart,' he said.

Acknowledgements

I should like to acknowledge the following publications, where some of the poems in this collection first appeared: *Landfall* ('Smiles like flowers come and go', 'Grand-daughter Polly Peaches', 'Christmas lament', 'Thoughts on a Sufi proverb', 'Uh huh'); *Listener* ('With all things and with all beings we are as relative', 'Sun o (2)', 'Monologue', 'Humming', 'Totem thoughts'); *Soho Square IV*, edited by Bill Manhire, Bridget Williams Books, 1991 ('Irises'); *Peace Link*, September 1991 ('The bomb-aimer over Baghdad . . .').

I should also like to acknowledge the role of the University of Auckland and, more specifically, members of the Department of English, Professors Jackson and Wendt, and Sebastian Black, for no small assistance during my nine months as Literary Fellow for 1991 — without which this manuscript would not have been born!

In addition, I acknowledge the help of Juliet R. Adams of Christchurch, Hal Smith of Dunedin, for putting me on track with historical information relating to the 'Maid of Orleans' and the poem 'Irises', and last but not least Shirley Grace for providing me with a writing refuge at Pakiri, east of the bustling farming community of Wellsford, and for taking the cover photograph. Thanks also to Mel and Beryl Dowson of Wellsford, for giving me food and shelter overnight, and to Barry Lowden, the rural delivery (RD4) person, for giving me a lift into town to get provisions.

Hone Tuwhare
Birkdale
January 1992

Front words: Monologue

I like working near a door, I like to have my work-bench
    close by, with a locker handy.

Here, the cold creeps in under the big doors, and in the
    summer hot dust swirls, clogging the nose. When the
    big doors open to admit a lorry-load of steel, conditions
    do not improve. Even so, I put up with it, and wouldn't
    care to shift to another bench, away from the big doors.

As one may imagine this is a noisy place with smoke rising,
    machines thumping and thrusting, people kneading,
    shaping, and putting things together. Because I am nearest
    to the big doors I am the farthest away
    from those who have to come down to shout
    instructions in my ear.

I am the first to greet strangers who drift in through
    the doors looking for work. I give them as much information
    as they require, direct them to the offices, and
    acknowledge the casual recognition that one worker
    signs to another.

I can always tell the look on the faces of the successful
    ones as they hurry away. The look on the faces of the
    unlucky I know also, but cannot easily forget.

I have worked here for fifteen months.
    It's too good to last.
    Orders will fall off
    and there will be a reduction in staff.
    More people than we can cope with
    will be brought in from other lands:
    people who are also looking

for something more real, more lasting,
more permanent maybe, than dying . . .
I really ought to be looking for another job
before the axe falls.

These thoughts I push away, I think that I am lucky
    to have a position by the big doors which open out
    to a short alley leading to the main street; console
    myself that if the worst happened I at least would have
    no great distance to carry my gear and tool-box
    off the premises.

I always like working near a door. I always look for a
    work-bench hard by — in case an earthquake
    occurs and fire breaks out, you know?

Blackbird fly

I never thought to look behind the copper sheet hiding my fireplace.
Overturned and sprung, a mousetrap rests in the grate. But pulsing
there, a bird sat once. Of mice there is no sign, let alone the smell
of dead ones. Only dead glow-worms; a night emptied of stars. For if
you looked up the chimney, you couldn't see daylight. The chimney
curves away out of sight of itself.

It was a blackbird come:
a blackbird with a yellow beak wearing a light speckled undervest
with the sheen of it fading. It had blundered blindly down my
chimney and couldn't find its way up again, or out. I heard it
throbbing and threshing there behind the copper sheet which acts as
a sort of draught cut-off, with a heavy electric heater ensconced
in front of it. Of course I didn't know for sure where the sound
initially, was coming from as I have a tendency for deafness in my
left ear — which plays disorientating tricks on me, sometimes. But I
worked it out that it must've been a fledgling which had fallen out
of a nest lodged in an out-of-the-way part of the chimney.

This bird could fly! When I pulled the copper sheet away, the bird
and I cautiously studied each other in absolute stillness for what
seemed ages; and I, fearful of being attacked, and readying myself
to shield my eyes with my hands, was suddenly relieved when the bird
in a flash, sought height as well as light thudding vainly against
the upper pane of my window, tapping futilely at it, and blunting
its nose.

I raised the bottom half of the window wide, and invited the bird
to become a Prince again of its more natural allies of air and sun.
Well, it couldn't bear to lower itself. I knew then that it had
given in to a more ancient dread of predatory enemies, walking,
crawling, hurtful — and tied to earth.

I drew the curtain around it to restrain movement. I climbed up on
    a chair and stretched. I placed a gentle hand over the bird, and
    with the other, reached under the curtain trapping its thin legs.
    I felt its tiny heart beating hard. I stepped down, and gestured it
    away through the opening with a gruff: this one's on me.

It felt good to see the blackbird curve away in flight and up again,
    banking tightly to the right, and clamping itself to a bare branch
    on a neighbour's apple tree, where it immediately began stocktaking.

There is an old Maori saying which goes: if a bird flies around inside
    your house, it's not there merely to chomp up all your house-flies.
    I did not think to ask my feathered visitor if it was a bearer of
    bad news. It would have died if I hadn't sensed its need for a hand.
    It flew away having regained the captaincy of its skills in the air,
    its departure marked only by the meticulous diligence the blackbird
    took in ridding itself of soot — a light dusting of freedom from me
    for an amateur chimney-sweep — and I hope, without prejudice.

Bird of prayer

On the skyline
a hawk
languidly typing
a hunting poem
with its wings.

Smiles like flowers come and go

Do you believe in G—D? you ask.

When I think of your asking, my head hurts.
And to a hinterland part of me sometimes, you're
a pain. Mostly though, you charm me, enthrall, with your
own special passions of sincerity, of truth embedded
in the magic koha-envelopes of poetry you post me.

My thought today is an enlargement of a grin as I prophesy
a certainty: the Coming of the red camellia blooms of the
japonica, for instance. Thorny and jersey-grabbing
the slender leafy arms of the japonica juggle small green
squat-shaped quinces in the wind right outside
the scratched frame of my kitchen window.

Tena koe. Kei te pehea koe? japonica asks, with an indrawn
hiss of nipponese perfection. I bow, clap my bare heels
together returning the Maori words of greetings in precise
deutschen Akzent — alle Vokale haargenau — all the vowel
sounds are bang on . . . And

I recall, only minutes ago, a dying rose released five
of its petals all in one go, drawing attention like a magnet
to their cushioned fall. A hushed achievement. No fanfare
or regret. And no flowers, please.

I am thinking of marketing, Fallen Rose-Petal Tea.

I think also of the red hedge-clippers lying on the sill
of my packed workroom, just waiting to snap and snip
away at something — reminding me to discard limp flowers

and to refill the flower-vases that are milk bottles.
I see yet, white cascading stars of fragrant blooms come
spilling over to the sunny side of my kind neighbour's
jasmine hedge. My fingers itch for the red hedge-clippers.

All these things crowd in on me as my thoughts come
back to you gently, with clarity . . . And I think, I think
smiles are fugitive, and unlike the forever ones, their
impermanence constant as the movement and boil of clouds.

My smiles are displaced; work-lines furrow my brow.
And on my brow you dance, cartwheel, do a Yoga-stand on
one foot; my fingers flexed above a favourite pen.

I am the Wild One, I am Incompetent Omnipotent,
the Immanent Will — o, and any other little thing One
might like to call One . . . but —

Shhh! I am writing: A–R–O–H–A   (love)

A view from a house in Rue Balguerie

Perching high on the crater-rim west of the town the sun lowers
    itself out of sight and behind the only car access-road
    over the saddle. What can I say if others shake their
    heads, regarding my point of view merely as banal — an
    imagician's view of the sun, settling down for the night?

    But this is one out of the bag: a one-off. Our eyes sucked
    in by the afterglow, we ponder the wonder of clouds up there
    yonder — by thunder — dressing up and trying on a flash line
    of rags in silver and gold, purple and black; a grey kind
    of slow-moving cavalcade of smudged eye-brows, lifting and
    sidling into the spot-light, showing off — and moving on.

Why, even now other lovers — replete with the sun and love and
    in a direct line with the western crater-saddle going right
    the way through to Westport — are gazing intently far out
    across the Tasman Sea, watching the sun's lower lip sizzle
    the waves in a steamy kiss. More clouds are born. Back east
    stars are crowding in through the back door and fanning out.
    The wobbly gem-prickly bracelet lying slackly

    on the pulsing wrist of the harbour has been
    consigned to deeper waters. Tomorrow morning, that impudent
    demi-god Maui will restore it freshly to the light of
    day after flipping a huge golden coin in the air, and into
    a slow controlled orbit.

To the north, the evening star, Tawera, makes a curtsy; da daa . . .
    Bell-bird and kiss-chirping fantails have snuggled deeper
    into their feather duvets. I go inside. A residual warmth
    remains in the enclosed glassed-in day room as you draw
    the heavy drapes, put a match to the kindling. The stove

is cast iron, as rotund as my belly. Already it is begin-
ning to chuckle and snap its hungry chops at the wood, flame
enveloped, releasing a blue mythology of embalmed energy —
the memory of tree-tops thrusting skywards higher and higher
seeking their essence in the moistness of clouds — the wind
running seductive fingers through the leaves.

Sun o (2)

Gissa smile Sun, giss yr best
good mawnin' one, fresh 'n cool like

yore still comin' — still
half in an' half outa the lan'scape?

An' wen yore clear of that eastern rim
of hills an' tha whole length of tha

valley begins to flood wit yr light, well
that's wen I could just reach out 'n stroke

tha pitted pock-marked pores of yr shiny
skin an' peel ya — just like a orange, right

down to yr white under-skin, but I wouldn't
bite ya — well, not until the lunch-bell goes

at noon wen I can feel ya hot an' outa reach
an' balanced right there — above my head.

C'mon, gissa smile Sun.

Well — I — never

Waist deep and crouched down by the pool-side
    the rocks looked solemn; there were five of them
    hid bald and tight-knuckled in reflective shadows.
    On the surface of the pool itself, a narrowing
    carpet of light pointing to the moon was laid on
    for us until it fractured when we got into it.
    For a while, it looked as if the moon was going
    to stay still, forever.

Well, just beyond this encircling haven we could hear
    the turbulence of water in the river gushing and
    very happy to lower its level below my chin just
    so I could keep my head above water. My body
    immersed, I can feel your exciting ballerina legs
    draped over my shoulders at the knees — heels
    threshing and in no way consigned to inaction like
    a flop-eared Dali watch — my mouth making a junction
    with your hair, your pubic mount of Eden.

Now as you gurgle your joy we drown in violent scrummage
    and squirm of bodies lassooed by a whirling cosmic
    string of sperm engraced by and enlacing the pearly
    gate. Well, for a moment everything is stopped.

When I shoot up again for air the pulsing cry of crickets
    telephoning each other seems to obtrude above all else
    except for the slide-fit of you bearing down as I stretch
    up up on my toes from the pool-bed/o, a real Space Dick/
    and counting only four dark sinewy rocks awash now
    in disturbed water, the other engulfed by your thighs —
    your legs hooked around my hips, my back, like a giant
    rosary as you begin chanting a mantra, a benediction, and
    pouring beads of sweet poison or something into my deaf
    ear and leaving me a-splutter . . . and o, breath-tooken.

Kitten

the phone didn't ring
yesterday.

it never even looked like
starting

and no letters've come
today, either — except

a stray kitten

i have given it milk;
it has adopted me

we've had a brief talk
about his mum? his dad?

you might say it was
a one-sided chat about cats:

but nothing's come of it

kitten knows only two
words and one of them is:

slurp

it is making love to my
feet: it understands

my loneliness . . . miaow?

The bomb-aimer over Baghdad remembers
his childhood as the best
kid in the block on
Star Wars machines

I remember where it all started. Every Pay Day
    I'd wait impatiently for me Mum to get back
    from work. She wd come in real stuffed and
    throw a bag of chippies at my head. Catch,
    she'd say to me and I would just let the chips
    in the colourful bag fall to the floor where
    I'd stamp on it screaming: GIVE ME MY POCKET
    MONEY NOW! But then I'd tone my voice down
    to a soft whine: aw, I've waited long enough . . .
    So, she'd say: what's the problem, Billy, huh?

Well, while me Mum's snuffling round inside her
    purse for small change, I'd grab a piece of
    paper with a ten printed on it and rush out
    the door — her voice: hey, you come back here!
    ghosting me — to the Games Parlour where I'd get
    a pocketful of change pushing other kids aside —
    some of them are broke by now, anyway — and
    standing before my favourite games machines I'd
    salute it: STAR WARS! And–and–and

    delicately
    I'd manipulate the buttons with alert fingers
    caressing & juddering & almost jerking myself
    off in the excitement as I stalk my static no-
    where-to-go-target on the ground, codenamed:
    Jello. And–and–and, AND

BINGO! I'd scream — and everyone in the whole
      world watching me on screen wd applaud my skill
      in eliminating yet another mother-fucken-bomb-
      shelter hiding: WHO'S-FUCKEN-SANE (hus sein,
      get it?) and everyone — I mean, everyone wd
      shout: RIGHT ON, BILLY, RIGHT ON . . .

That's where it got a start; at the Games Parlour.
C'mon, World War III, I'm ready 'n . . . waitin' for ya.
Eeeee — Yup!

Monika

Tonight I observe you've had your blond hair
shorn. A criminal act. I'm confused.
But I congratulate you — and myself for noticing.
I order a beer downing it with relish.

Mochtest du noch eins, Johannes?

Ja bitte, Monika. Wordless, I drink the second glass
to your eyes opened wide and lit up. I drink
to the expressive lift and fall of your arm
and shoulder; the silken loiter and tilt of your
breasts mouthing not one tiny word of apology
for their insolence, the proud sensual hint
of line and bulk —

Sorry? I ask. You look at me in wonderment.
I've not caught a single word you've said!

And this evening, in the cosy Yugoslav Kneipe in
Nachod Strasse, I greet Horst, Auto Mechanic
working for VOLVO. I say Guten Abend, to Frau
Richter and her dog, and a couple of others whose
faces I've got to know after a few visits.

Monika, you enfold all with your vivacity and élan.
In a twinkle of an eye, a wave of an invisible
wand, re-make of each, a fashion Princess all aglow,
a tipsy king — on his night off as a Maintenance
Fitter on the Lake Ferry, a Frog changing quite rapidly
into a Prince (me) — a fugitive Queen with a spark-up
singing a Country & Western old one:

Theer goes mah reason for wantin' you, theer goes mah ev'ra THA-ING

And the Queen, unable to go on, is just about ready now
to do a royal chunder (not a dance) abandoning all,
Her Crown, Her Common Lover, Her Royal Ring —

Monika, Monika, you defer to each their own private
space to savour or survey hunger or thirst
nail-polish or navel, friend, future enemy or lover.

Johannes, you like strong German beer, ja?

Ja! Strong German women, too, mit hairy mussels
smoked Aale, raw herrings: wunderbar!
Bring mir Alles, bitte — mit Salat. Ich liebe dich.

Ja, ja . . . Johannes. Ist schon gut.

Imp

(to Juliet)

Wind furrowed are
the sea pastures where
white horses prance
your eyes merry me
the corners of the
heart a mouth
uptilted

Grand-daughter Polly Peaches

There's no time between
now and my transition
to say goodbye to you.

Goodbye? Waste of time.

There's not enough room left
on the upturned butter-box
for your impetuous body
to come crashing alongside.

Oh, you'll damn me forever
for being kingly and remote —
for not granting you
a special audience: No

you may NOT sit on my knees.
You don't KNOW how swiftly
they grow numb when blood
flow is cut off.

It's good out here in the sun.

But, there IS a special need for me
to concentrate on each cell
and tube of me; listen to them
burble, and squeak, and sigh: All
systems go; or, just going,
thanks. And soon, soon

I shall be as deaf as stone
to all but the Hallelujah voices
of starched and whitened angels

swingin', 'Abide with me' with
a tasty back-up by ol' Satchmo Louis
Armstrong, white handkerchief, mute
and horn — and when those Saints come
stompin' in, well, I ask you —

Now, be a good child and piss off, will ya?

Pith off, y'thelf, Gwun-dud.

Shadow

Implicit above all and
as pervasive as the Duende
of Federico García Lorca
is the sense that I must tread
the liveliest and loneliest
of measures on my way
to Rarohenga cocking a snook
at the shadow of my creative
bones, thinning.

And clearly
I should be real gone when
I reach there — the place where
I am not — except for my end-words
and that, surely, is a beginning.

Thoughts on a cold winter morning

I've not kept a tally of how many times I've riz
        from a lonely bed to grapple with my love-muscle —
        revise a song for you, o how many times now, Liz?

Verily there are as many melancholies as there are
        common places. For a long time now I've been living
        in the basement of your I-don't-want-to-know dreams
        rent free, thoroughly absorbed with flesh-fantasies
        and an unerring sense of direction and foreknowledge
        of just where the hunched figure of the man in your
        pink canoe is positioned; the mouse-fur

        I love to stroke; your tail a noodle snuggled
        into my tom cat's mouth, and slurped satisfyingly
        out of sight. But your fires are banked, foreclosing
        on me?

Things are more prosaic.
        My bladder is a clock with set habits. The pen is
        mightier than a catapult, and both pen & penis are
        performing a natural function this morning.
        I go outside waving my gristle around
        like a wand.

        I have a blue Super Bowl audience of millions
        snicker-tittering away as I arc an amber curve of
        liquid light over a tuft of grass discovering —
        long before Einstein — that light bends?

Stars recoil as I hum an ancient hymnal:

'. . . there's a rainbow round my
shoulder, and the skies are hum hum hum . . .'

It's 6:19 a.m. on a cold winter morning. I can't see
    the Cross. It should be hanging upside down now; but
    the Pointers are there, clear as balls — um, bells?

Tour bus minutiae, and commentary: West Berlin, 1985

I have felt the bite & crunch of winter winds, the sudden
stir of snow hunched around the corner waiting to pounce
on you, I'm envigoured by it. It's called: Berliner Luft:
Duft, Duft, dufte! Loverly.

Dog-lovers walk their pets home, anxious to complete
the chore quickly, a marvel of detachment & poise as the dog
pisses or shits. When new snow lies white on the ground,
the nature-mess that dogs make is easier to see and avoid.

There are over a hundred thousand dogs registered
in Berlin. The City Authorities are sympathetic.
Two hundred and fifty thousand trees have been planted.

Despite the generosity of statistics, there are canine
territorial disputes over the third tree. Tribal Elders
from my Dog Tribe — Ngati Kuri — will send a mediator
to Geneva, me. It's not a piddly matter.

Every tree has been given a number which I find phantastisch!
You may rendezvous with the beautiful Dame from East Berlin
unter den Linden tree Nummer 2231 Eisenberger Strasse.
On the Wannsee border-bridge, a Spy Exchange Service —
Spionageaustauschdienst — is in place.

Dead leaves, which carpet drain and pathway, are cleared away
by City Council workers who come from Italy and Türkei.
Five tons of dog-dung is collected every day.

Bottled bio-gas from such a rich source is exported.
Gas ovens at Dachau & Auschwitz have been made redundant.
A taped recording of mixed doggy-barks is enclosed with each
bottle. I'm not impressed . . . Doggy-bark recording is a dubious
practice.

On the Lietzensee Ufer the trees are stark and still. A ridge
of snow rests along the tops of their nobbly, snaky branches,
their dark winter bareness, fattened and enhanced. On the frozen
lake, voices go up in steam — to the hiss of skates, sluicing . . .

Inside the warm pub on Nachod Strasse a dog comes in wagging
its owner, Sabine, on the end of a leash. Sabine orders a coffee,
unwinds her scarf. The dog sits down by her feet. Helmut, a Berliner,
greets her with tongue-in-cheek: 'Sabine, kommen Sie hier bei Fuss?'

Dear Brown Bear City, I love you. Ach ja! You're a bloody wonder-
ful ache.

pray
er: to my autumn deity, gosh

when i speak
your name,
gosh

i'm filled
with effulgence
awe, an old pain —
a banked inhibition

that is fire —
with a yellow carpet
drawn over its eyes
as leaves smother

the mother that
is earth smelling
sharply of decay
and of oils — biting
dryly into the lungs —
and the lungs

whistling
opening out newly
to lacerate spears
of smoke lancing
healing them: o

you plea
sure me, gosh:
thank you very mulch

for stooking my sighs and raking
          my breath away like
                    like leaves gosh:
               like leaves?

Humming

It is a house to be constructed with care
    for it has no confining walls
    thus permitting expansion: vertical

    growth is not inhibited for there
    is no limit to the height of the ceiling
    stretching to heaven. This house
    can endure given a chance, that's
    for sure . . . H m m m m

But since it is of earth its foundations may be
    built of sand: and because there are
    no confining walls this fragile house
    of love may be seen as layers of light
    and colour — a feeling tone — warm, purple
    orange grey hot and cold with lots of blue
    and yellow to make it green — green
    and predictable . . . H m m m m

Fleshed out though, this house of love isn't
    ageless, but ages old. It has form; contour.
    It has presence; a brilliant arc uniting
    heaven and hell; love-thoughts in pursuit of
    a physical expression — a noisy, gloppy
    proclamation —

        Aha   Aha — Aha — Aha   Aha

    . . . and horses, huffing and pounding into
    the straight, riders snarling, cruel whips
    flailing — the anguish of stretched leather
    reeking sweetly of sweat . . . And reason? Ahh.

Reason is a hunchback of irrelevance backing
quietly out the door.

But where are the flowers — the select flowers
     of endearment, soul-food to dazzle the heart?

     O, they're here, all right: there, there
     and THERE . . . H m m m m

*With all things and with all beings we are as relative**

Sunlight through the window falls
    on a pot-plant just breaking out
    in flower on the table.

    For a moment the flower
    is itself, complete.
    Which, of course, is a fiction.
    The flower gets its nourishment
    from the sun, and from me.

I will sing to it — chat it up.
    I will give it porridge-water to drink
    thin and cloudy. And today I might even
    celebrate its birth with an aria
    flamboyant and breathy.

    If I am as constant as the sun
    the moon and tide, the flower will die
    and I shall will it to bud again.

    Ten thousand times live to die; die
    and live again. And this is normal, quite
    acceptable; timely.

But who accepts as easily
    his own brief life as ebb and flow?
    As part of waxing and waning?
    As part of the coming and going away
    Of sun and flower, moon and tide?

*The title of the poem is a proverb attributed to Chief Seattle, North American.

Hail to sophistry, the cult of the individual, hooray

The call was so clear and the vision he had strong that Bonesy just had to slap on his sandals and go up to the top of Mount Cyanide where he met the Great Chemist — who wanted an offer, a sacrifice; could he, Bonesy, accommodate Him?

He spent a while up there hallucinating with the Great One, and when he came down off it he was very happy. He was clutching a couple of tablets which he turned into hundreds and thousands — just like that — and the people loved him for it and waited for their portion of the sweet tiny balls together with his final instructions.

'Take a palmful immediately with lotsa water,' he said and they did because they knew that he, Bonesy, was speaking to them with the voice of Authority the Great Chemist had passed on to him.

They were pained   indeed contorted — for the taking of it, and died haggardly, inexcusably, one by one with eyes forgiving him as he Bonesy sauntered over to his private jet called: Heavenly Wings:

'See ya all up there — for sure,' he muttered. Well hadn't he chosen them himself?

But a few were left walking around in a daze, with spew all over the front of their shirts, feebly shaking their fists at him. Up ahead some had even lain down on the runway to stop him. He swung the nose of Heavenly Wings off the runway and into the sparse grass. He gunned the motor and the ride became bumpy. An impudent rabbit came out of a hole in front of the jet, blew each nostril separately with a forepaw — how dare you — turned, and ran off, tiny white arse-tuft bobbing.

Then a wheel ran into the rabbit hole and the left wing dipped into the ground. The ground took it off neatly at the hip as the jet spun and flipped over on its back. He heard splashings like someone relieving himself. Angry faces were now looking down at him hanging there — his world turned suddenly upside down by a bunny. Their mouths curling and froth-stained, he could just hear them:

'Give us back our Faith — our 11% — you monster, you cheat! Give us back our lives —' and rocks thudded against the perspex but didn't break it.

Then the people with spew on their fronts ran away and for a while there was just a silence that was heaven; until Bonesy smelled the kerosene, and heard it again sloshing freely on the ground.

A tiny flame came out of the wing which could no longer be heaven-borne. The flame took its time building a smoke from which would grow a bigger flame. He couldn't lift a finger. He couldn't stop anything. Not even the river of shit he could feel running down his back.

Everyone went to ground as the jet burst into a great sheet of flame and seconds later their hearing went as the explosion caught up with them. Emerging out of the sound-shock a lonely woman's voice sobbed: 'God forgive him.' Another voice — incredulous — cried: 'What? Your husband and child are back there — in the church — all twisted up and dead.'

'GODDAMN HIM, THEN!' she shouted.

'Yeah, that's the ticket! Good for you and good for us — what's left!'*

*Prose-poem based on Jim Jones' People's Temple Movement, which began, sporadically, in 1955 and ended dramatically at Jones' 824-acre outpost in Guyana, where followers of the Movement including women, children and old people were induced (some say coerced) to take a drink out of a tub of strawberry-ade laced with tranquillisers and cyanide.

Nine hundred and eleven people died from this 'holy drink' administered by nurses and doctors.

Uh huh

Late today Hilda came early for a pre-performance drink with
    me before going on to our first-night show together. A knock
    on the door and there she was
    dressed in some kind of see-through boudoir-black French lace
    that is usually worn over the head like tents by majestic flotilla
    of Spanish dames.

The black lacy stuff caressed Hilda's body like a snake. When
    she stood in the doorway with the light behind her I could
    feel the warmth of the late afternoon sun poking hot fingers
    through her dress: jesus Hilda, I breathed, protuberant eyeballs,
    Hilda, I said, are you really wearing pants under that?
    Stooping swiftly she grabbed the hem of her dress, straightened
    up, and like the ingénue she is held it up to her eyes like a
    veil. See? she said.

Uh huh . . .
And right there and then, like a revelation I was converted
    to the ancient belief from Genesis — you know the one — from
    erection to resurrection? And of Jesus.
    Not the juvenile Jesus showing off to his elders in tight jeans
    but an older one, the sun a golden trumpet orbiting around
    his head and hitting brassy tremolos in high 'C' and Him with
    long hair down to his shoulders, bushy beard and twinkling
    eyes — like Karl Marx who is for real — like REAL? — burned nose
    peeping from a bed of hair.
    And Hilda, Hilda, I said — fearful of being upstaged — you won't
    have to speak ONE word of poetry tonight. You stun me.

Ah-agh, she said, black silk lace lisping down as she poked a
    sparkling finger of admonishment, straight up. You're not
    honest. If you lust after me — say it . . . Now pour me a drink.
    And I did:
    for me.

Christmas lament

Christmas comes and Xmas goes
and once again we're exhorted
to celebrate
the commercialised phenomenon

of the Holy Kehua's sneaky visit
to Mary on earth. Verily
an immaculate con job by starving
Mediterranean & Gulf scribes

gone high on wilderness air and
desert weed — their inventive
writings a mine-field of poetry
but really of no consequence

whatever, to starving Palestinian
women, old people, children
blasted out of their home-land,
Palestine.

Oh well, Christmas comes and Xmas
goes — o, dinga bloody ding. Now
just pass me that jar of puha and
mussels, e hoa. Holy Juices! I can

settle for that kind of Passover;
develop a special gut-pain of joy
and hate, perhaps love . . . perhaps,
for the rigidities of dogma & rote

— an ideological pus; a bloat
and swelling of contradictions.

Israelis! You have betrayed the Holy
Land. You have crucified it. Your pockets
stuffed with American dollars, you have
become the new Goliath of Strut!

What new Messiah from Gaza, from Aramaea
will rise up to stone you and clean out
the temples of the Holy Land? And who will
piss on your betrayers, the loathsome

moneyed-men of Zion, ay?

Okay, let's start again — from here

Maybe it was the low seductive caress of a melody
    in a minor key played by the flautist at that
    pub on the Peninsula?

Or perhaps it was some kind of fish-bone or trip-wire
    catching me in the throat in a sort of mid-reverie
    blues — as the sky drew on some dark second-hand
    clothes fraying badly at the sleeves — the rain
    bouncing merrily off the concrete? Whatever.
    But when I began

        to reconstruct a song that was once an unvoiced
        blues reverie, my eyes gave me away — my face
        a soggy blotter. And then
        When I began articulating each word carefully
        with an exaggeration that made my friends shuffle
        and cough forgiving me, I gave up; and as they turned
        from me, I heard them vowing loudly: T'hell with him —
        pure corn . . . Don't give him any more gin.

Two hours have gone since my throat got tripped up on the
    fish-bone-wire in there. I feel good after several
    cups of strong tea sugar and full-creamed milk
    with a dunked dog-biscuit or two inside me. But what
    was it, exactly? Not a good time to go into it.

        The ground's damp and steamy and the sky naked
        in its blueness, with the sun exposing itself and
        pissing skin-cancer down on everybody coming awake
        and in occupation of the turning, lit-up half
        of the world ball?

        I can feel the heat-shimmer rising from the tar seal.
        I can feel again.

You have to come first before you can go

Oh it's true — it's true. And it gets harder at
    night, thinking of you. Harder still appease
    an appetite more constantly in bud with your
    comings rather than your goings. For it has
    no useful name except, love; seemingly
    old-fashioned, and imprecise.

And if the sky were unpeopled — the stars and planets
    have a falling out with it — it would make
    a memorable mark; like my nail-gouged buttocks
    that you've tinctured pink, the shattered bed
    frame — mute evidence that we'd got into it.
    You'll just have to cut your nails, or wear
    boxing gloves, and may I say, in a reserved
    judgment, that our exulting most moving parts
    are compatible?

And you, you
    at the most extreme sou'westerly end now
    of spun kilometres — to whom phone calls dialled
    around midnight might assuage — in return
    call down on me a good night; a dark warm coat
    to nudge into and hug.

Fish soup, s'il vous plaît

My eyes are barbed-out and gaffed
by the jiggly sun-tints bouncing off
the waves just out taking a gentle early
evening stroll, at the start of a very
fine dinner beginning with a succulent
bouillabaisse at the Wharf Restaurant
on the anniversary of our second meeting,
to be precise, (when it was truly a more
thorough rediscovery of each other — and
great fucking) the dinner ending

in a glut of plum puddings we can't put
away but take home hot anyway, in a couple
of plastic boats, with ice-cream dobs
melting around them as I juggle them
deftly with hot hands while you drive us
home madly to put them away in the fridge
for a rainy morrow: and then abandoning
Mosaic laws and

acts of neutrality, we turn openly
to each other and to the holier Order
of Fitter and Turner, steam-puffs and welded
joints, stuffing ourselves up with each
other in a fitting end to Holy Feast Day.

Thoughts on a Sufi proverb

A long time ago I was an atom. A one-ness in two, superbly put together.
Full of potential, I was close to my essence. I died as an atom and
progressed to another form. I became a stone just off the melt. I was
cooling off.

I died as a stone and became a water-plant. As a plant, I learned to trap
and eat meat. I died as a plant and became fish. As a fish I grew
wings flying low over the heaving waters. Then I aspired to circle
high above greening turret-lands.

When I died as a plant, another branch of me I liked grew legs and
crawled out of the sea — on all fives. Or was it sixes and sevens?
No matter, I had arms, legs, and two hands with which I learned
to pick up stones, sharpen a stick.

That other flying branch of me tried to pick out my eyes. They mocked me
for not choosing a flying career. I ignored the jibes, ducking out of
sight to avoid danger. I learned to throw stones. And soon, with a
developed accuracy I could bring down my tormentors. I ate them feathers
and all, only learning later to save the feathers to adorn myself.

I progressed from a plant, and became animal. I died as an animal and
became man. Now . . . never did I grow less by dying, you understand?

I want to become stone again, but not of the kind that is as cold as the
forever night — the unlit side of the moon.
For a stone is as good a shape or form as any other. Compact and
smoothened to become a million whispering grains of sand just
crumbling quietly away to whatever ancestral dust; and all in
good time, too, precisely, and with a resigned elegance.

I have a small niggle. I am assailed by a recurrent thought that it is
a diminishment of the dignity of all our kind if we were to join
our common ancestor — the atom — with such unseemly and
precipitate haste.

Irises

(for Joan of Arc and Vincent)

Van Gogh's spiritual sister, Joan, dropped by today fisting a pea-
    nut butter jar full of tremulous irises. The irises were
    velvet-soft and purply; the fragile blooms showing off
    their centres which flared like peacock tail feathers
    or Hawaiian beach-shirts billowing on a clothes line. But
    some were in bud, closed down and private, like moths' wings
    on their day off.

In a warm room like this, said the Maid of Orleans, they'll open
    out — all of them, Have you got some water?

I turned the tap on and Joan filled the jar nearly to the top.
    I took it away from her and placed the irises on top of the
    radio where they trembled to the beat of the music.

Vincent thought you might like some fresh irises today, so I picked
    some from a garden full of them that he was trying to
    paint.

    Hey, I'm not complaining, I said; Nature, is art's finest
    lover, its best — and ONLY student. They're . . . exquisite, I said
    already in debit.

    Beauty doesn't make a thing of it, she said, they're just so . . .
    momently. I'd like a drink of water —

I can do better than that, I said, producing a glass into which
    I poured some dry red wine from a green bottle, and pressed
    from grapes off vines brought from Dalmatia and
    growing on dairy flats at Kumeu.
    I topped it up with cubistic water from the fridge discantating
    all the while, like a fussy guru — to take my mind off

Joan's suit of rough red cloth which I hoped would not
suddenly go up in flames, just now.

For Joan wasn't wearing her white armour made in Tours, a city
   famous for its armourers, or sword with five crosses on it
   and banner, on which was painted her own motto: JESUS MARIA.

Joan did not ride up on a fierce horse with cross eyes, muscles
   bunched, nostrils flaring. Instead, she came on a four-wheeled
   charger which purred when you turned the motor on. I don't know
   how she got away with it going through the lights at 130 K's,
   with the irises lolling around in the plastic jar on the seat
   beside her. A special messenger from the rainbow goddess,
   Aniwa-niwa? Hell, I'm in love with the world again.

Merci; and Kia ora, I said, handing her the glass of wine and water.
   In one go, I downed mine. But Joan rolled the first mouthful
   around for a while, before swallowing; Mon Dieu! she breathed,
   I can smell the wine, you, me, the irises — everything! Salut!

Back words: Totem thoughts

Coming in from the northern end of the pa, I ran slap-bang into my
ancestors. They were embracing; 'I thought it was you fellers,' I said as I
stepped back — after reading the inscription in English. I tried hard not to
sound triumphant. 'Christ, us fellers are everywhere, like . . . like Jesus
Rabbits,' I said, grinning.

Together, they formed a neat join on top of the arch. I had to squint up
at them, framed as they were by a hot afternoon sky with a lot of blue
showing, wisps of orange trailing. But my ancestors turned only to look
down at me, full-faced, cheek to cheek, eyebrows peaking.

She wore a moko on her chin, but that was all. She was seated between
his thighs with her legs wrapped around his hips in classical style (a style
not unknown to the Ngati Tarawhai carvers), her feet locked together
behind his back, twiddling her toes. She looked arch. I guessed she was
comfortable.

My male ancestor looked fearsome. He was tattooed on his buttocks as
well. He caught my eye — and held it (from the playing fields behind the
hospital, a cricket crowd erupted with applause, beer cans). He was
treating me now as if I was some kind of truant intruder — a Jack Nohi.*
He said: '. . . well, if the pa is NOT under attack, why don't you piss off,
then?'

Aw, heavy. But I didn't want to argue the toss. In point of fact, the pa
was about to be taken over — I am bound to say — by a GLIB
COMMERCIAL INTEREST. But who cares for that? For lovers — like my
ancestors — it was a period of supreme self-containment: a timely and
timeless happening — history, art, more sex, me.

I moved closer to the carved wooden supports of the archway, examining them for tiny tell-tale holes. For starters someone had already done a good paint job on them with a coat of red lead. I turned away. It was going to be another one of those days: boring. I turned to them again: 'We'll make it,' I said. 'On my feet you walk. Have a good day.'

*Jack Nohi — a common term applied to a person obsessively curious, persistent and tiresome in poking his or her nose into other people's private affairs.